Teenagers Learning strategies

By

Jagdish Yadav

Newbee Publication

Copyright © 2020 Jagdish Yadav

All rights reserved

No part of this book may be reproduced, or stored in a retrieval system, or transmitted in any form or by any means, electronic, mechanical, photocopying, recording, or otherwise, without written permission of the publisher.

LEARNING HOW TO LEARN

Contents

LEARNING HOW TO LEARN 1

LEARNING HOW TO LEARN: LEARNING STRATEGIES FOR TEENAGERS 8

  Preface 8

LEARNING

  What is learning?

OWNERSHIP IN LEARNING 17

ASSOCIATION ABILITY 21

CHUNKING 26

  How to chunk information? 27

MEMORY 30

ELABORATIVE REHEARSAL 32

MAINTENANCE REHEARSAL 34

PASSION 36

PERSEVERANCE 39

ACTIVE RETRIEVAL 43

SPACING 44

INTERLEAVING PRACTICE 45

NAPPING BETWEEN STUDIES 46

COOPERATIVE LEARNING 51

   Types of Cooperative Learning 52

DEBATE 55

DISCUSSION 59

DRAMATIC PLAY 61

TYPES OF DRAMATIC PLAY 62

EXPERIMENTAL LEARNING 64

INSTRUCTIONAL EFFECTIVENESS 66

LECTURE METHOD 68

PEER TEACHING 71

ROLE PLAYING 73

PEG WORD MNEMONICS 75

SLEEP 77

NOTES TAKING METHOD 79

MEMORY BOOSTING TECHNIQUES 80

GRIT 82

EXPLICIT REMEMBERING 87

INTERESTING APPLICATION OF LEARNING 91

LOW STAKE QUIZZING 98

SPACING OUT PRACTICE 102

POSITIVITY IN THE SURROUNDING 106

REFLECTION 111

  Advantages of Reflection 113

SPACE VISUALIZATION 115

AUDITORY PROCESSING 122

LEVEL OF AROUSAL 127

ORIENTATION 133

ATTENTION SPAN 137

How to Develop Your Attention Span 138

CONCEPT FORMATION 144

SOCIAL CONDUCT 147

INTERPERSONAL SKILLS 150

SELF EXPRESSION 152

Ways To Express Yourself Better 153

SELF CONTROL 157

SHARING/TURN TAKING 160

PROCASTINATION 162

PLAY 166

Advantages of playing 167

POSTURE 172

REHEARSAL 175

ORGANIZATION SKILLS 177

LEARNING STYLES   179

STUDY DURATION   181

CONCLUSION   184

LEARNING HOW TO LEARN: LEARNING STRATEGIES FOR TEENAGERS

Preface

We all go to primary school, and then we proceed to college. The few lucky ones among us make it to the university in their life's academic cycle. During this period of Learning, we come across a lot of information; while we retain some of that information, we throw others out of the window, as though we never knew about them.

I consider it strange that "our education system focuses basically on what we need to learn, but it never taught us how this learning process should take place. Neither does it empowers students with insight on how to retain the learned knowledge."

I firmly believe that the learning process itself is a big subject and should be taught in schools as a part of the curriculum, just as much as any other subject like Mathematics and Sciences. Doing a job without the proper tools makes it difficult. The job becomes more challenging and less enjoyable. This same principle applies to studies.

Unless we equip ourselves and our children with the right tools and methodology, we are bound to make the learning process difficult. Studying is not as complicated as it appears. Once you acquaint yourself with learning how to proceed right, studying becomes much more fun. A proper learning process requires adopting a plan, a procedure, a strong desire, and consistent practice. I aim to address this in this book so that students can engage the process in their school and the future since Learning never stops.

Human beings have survived over the years because of their ability to learn skillfully. And it is through this art of Learning that we have mastered ways to overcome potential dangers and build up houses. As we get more sophisticated, we have come to a stage where we are confronted with finding more ways to do more work in less time. Computers, mobile phones, and online businesses are some of them. In this process of evolution, we have mastered so many areas, but somehow, we still did not introduce our future generations to the proper ways of Learning.

We do not use the knowledge that we gain in school or colleges for everything we do in life. It is strange but true, and most of the college grads do not even remember one-quarter of the subjects' teachings from school or after four years of leaving college.

As a health professional who has studied Pharmacy and Occupational therapy with all medicine components, I have noted this flaw in the education system worldwide. Our schoolteachers sometimes give us some tips, while some learn from tuition classes, but they are related to the subjects taught by those people. This book treats several topics on strategies that are effective for an effective learning process. While it focuses on teenagers, just about anyone can learn a lot through reading it.

I want to dedicate this book to those students in India who work very hard in their board exams and higher secondary schooling. I understand your effort because I have been there before. Besides understanding your experiences, I have studied how to transform your learning level to a better standard. All you need is to acquire this is "an open heart and an interest to improvise."

LEARNING

Learning is a never-ending process. It is a gift that we all possess as a living creature. It is the process of using that gift that makes every person unique. The irony of our education system is that it does not teach "how to learn." If only we had this subject in our curriculum, it would make learning fun for the students. As an Occupational therapist, I have a habit of doing activity analysis. In this process of study, I tried to break the entire process into different components. We learn holistically, and there is no single way of learning how to learn. In this book, I shall enumerate and elaborate on elements that play a vital role in our learning process. If we understand these different components of Learning, we can improve our understanding significantly. This book is a self-help book for people of all ages.

What is learning?

According to Wikipedia, "Learning is the act of acquiring new knowledge or the process involved in modifying and reinforcing existing, knowledge, behaviors, skills, values, or preferences which may lead to a potential change in synthesizing information, depth of the knowledge, attitude or actions relative to the type and range of experience."

Learning does not happen all at once, but it also banks on previously acquired knowledge. To that end, education is "a process rather than a collection of factual and procedural knowledge." Learning produces changes in the organism, and the changes made are relatively permanent. Through education, we acquire a better understanding that stays with you forever. Isn't that interesting?

In the case of humans, human Learning (may) occurs as part of education, personal development, schooling, or training. It should be goal-oriented and facilitated by motivation. The study about how Learning happens has a broad part in psychology, specifically, under educational psychology, neuropsychology, learning theory, and pedagogy. From these areas of psychology, we learn that Learning may occur because of habituation or classical conditioning, seen in many animal species. It also occurs because of more complex activities such as play, seen only in relatively intelligent animals.

Learning may happen consciously or without conscious awareness. It is, unlike other aversive events, cannot be avoided nor escaped; and hence is also known as learned helplessness. Merely looking at a legibly written text, in a language you understand, makes you start reading the book immediately; your eyes glance through it. You cannot see and not read. That is what happens when we learn; it happens voluntarily sometimes, but involuntarily most times. Putting your hand mistakenly in a bucket of hot water teaches you that the water is hot and that hot water can be unfriendly to your body. It all happens automatically. There is evidence for human behavioral Learning happening prenatally, in which habituation has been observed as early as 32 weeks into gestation) indicating that the central nervous system is sufficiently developed and primed for Learning and memory to occur very early in development."

There is a reference of prenatal education in the Indian Epic Mahabharata where the son of Arjuna (Abhimanyu) has mastered a skill of breaking into the enemies' rank named Charkravhu while he was in his mother's womb. However, he learned the strategy to break in, but he could not know how to get out, as his mother dozed while listening to Arjuna's narration of the potential plan.

You may assume that story is an old (doubtful) legend. Well, here is something interesting, according to current theory, in the human brain, a typical neuron collects signals from others through a host of delicate structures called dendrites. The neuron sends out spikes of electrical activity through a long, thin stand known as an axon, which splits into thousands of branches. At the end of each branch, a structure called 'synapse' converts the activity from the axon into electrical effects that inhibit or excite activity in the connected neurons. When a neuron receives excitatory input that is sufficiently large compared with its inhibitory input, it sends a spike of electrical activity down its axon. Ultimately Learning occurs by changing the effectiveness of the synapses so that the influence of one neuron on the other changes.

In conclusion, we learned in this chapter that Learning is a process that starts as early as the existence in any living thing. While we have had legends accounting to proofs of acquired knowledge from the fetal phase of life, science itself has asserted the credibility of the legend. Worthy of note is the fact that there is no one way to learning.

OWNERSHIP IN LEARNING

While we focused on what learning is in the previous chapter, we shall take a more in-depth look into the ownership in learning in this chapter. Taking ownership, as you know, implies standing up and taking responsibility for a task or project. Sometimes taking ownership will just mean being accountable for a project within your job description. Ownership is the level of investment a learner has in learning. In simple terms, it is helping students take control of their education—one of the most significant challenges with many students. I mean, one of the factors that debar them from effective learning is having control over their education process. Being in control of your education does not mean paying for the fees or determining which school you go to. Being in control has to do with your psychological position over your studies.

Any conversation about student ownership in school would be incomplete without the mention of John Dewey's assertions. It was his book, 'Democracy and Education' (published in 1916), that helped us see the connection between student involvement and students' ownership. According to Dewey, the type of activities that stimulate real involvement "gives pupils something to do, not something to learn; and the doing is of such a nature as to demand thinking or the intentional noting of connections; learning results naturally." It is a fact that we all notice in our day to day chores. We sometimes look for information in the newspaper, and after reading it, we see we have learned a few more things which we never thought we would know, initially before reading the paper. In this circumstance, we are in control of the education we got from the article.

Combining student ownership and literacy needs can lead to meaningful student involvement. Students must feel connected, engaged, and meaningfully involved when they go to school or college. They must feel in control. This integration is challenging but not impossible and must be addressed jointly by different professionals and needs partnership with parents. It is observed that students get better grades where "there is a logical integration between schools and parents." This integration puts a student in charge of the learning process, and they can set their goals and devise their strategies to meet them.

It also broadens students' sense of responsibility, and they initiate a discussion with parents at home and with teachers at school. They learn to dream and communicate among their peers, and this kicks in the learning process without much effort.

"If we are not keen about learning and we think it is someone else's responsibility, then we are not prepared for learning."

In conclusion, having ascertained earlier that learning can happen impulsively or deliberately, we learned in this chapter that for the effective learning process, students must be allowed to have a sensation of possession over (and especially) decisions about their academics. Parents and guardians must work together to ensure that the child feels connected to the academic choices they make. The result of this is that the child can work determinedly toward the same purposeful target as the parent to learn more and achieve results.

ASSOCIATION ABILITY

Learning is all about making connections and associations. The ability to learn is like a mortar in the making of a building. We learn new things by adhering the latest information to previously acquired ones. It seems to be the particular reason why some children do better than others in their studies. Those children who received adequate stimulation and chances of exploration in early childhood (which is a critical period for brain development) are good learners and do better. So, if the foundation is right and healthy, children become good and efficient learners as they associate things better.

Associative learning is a process by which we learn an association between two stimuli, or a behavior and a stimulus. It is the ability to learn and remember the relationship between unrelated items such as the name of someone we have met in a restaurant or the smell of deodorant. Each day we learn and remember a variety of additional information from the names of new people we meet to the best food at a restaurant. This information is first acquired and strengthened through a process called consolidation and gets stored in long-term memory.

The structures of the medial temporal lobe are essential for this ability to acquire new long-term memories for facts and events. The cell in the hippocampus provides healthy learning-related patterns of neural activity that participate in the initial formation of new associative memories. It is important to note that because these changes can occur before, at the same time after learning, these findings suggest that there may be gradual recruitment of a network of hippocampal neurons during the formation of new associative memories.

Associative learning occurs when you learn something based on a new stimulus. There is a very famous example. I am sure you must have heard of Ivan Pavlov's use of dogs to demonstrate that a catalyst, such as the ringing of a bell, leading to a reward, such as food, ensures the cycle of stimulus to reward expectation. There are two types of associative learning.

1. Classical conditioning, such as in Pavlov's dog.

2. Operant conditioning or the use of reinforcement through rewards and punishments.

Classical Conditioning

Classical conditioning involves the use of a stimulus — such as a bell in Pavlov's experiments — that is paired with a reward, resulting in salivation in the expectation of receiving food. Over repeated trials, the conditioned stimulus causes learning. By contrast, repeated instances without compensation lead to the abolition of the behavior.

Operant Conditioning

B.F. Skinner's experiments involve the use of a schedule of reinforcements, or rewards, and punishments until the behavior is learned. For instance, if the dog were to hear the bell and step on a lever, it would receive the dog biscuit, the reward. Alternatively, if the dog were to step on the lever when the bell does not ring and gets a shock — a positive punishment — that would shape behavior in the opposite direction. A negative sentence, by contrast, would be to take away something, such as a biscuit if the dog barks.

Non-associative Learning

Most animals show some degree of non-associative learning. It means they change their response to a stimulus without association with positive or negative reinforcement. Animals frequently subjected to a stimulus will often become habituated to that stimulus–they will show a reduction or total elimination of response to a stimulus without positive or negative reinforcement. If you poke them, sea slugs will curl inwards. However, if you poke them repeatedly, the response will become less and less extreme until they do not withdraw at all. When presented with a novel stimulus, such as an electric shock, the sea slugs will recover their withdrawal response to poking. This phenomenon in which the habituation disappears is, conveniently, known as dishabituation.

This chapter simply explains how favorable conditions are needed to spur the right actions and mindset.

CHUNKING

Chunking is another excellent aid in learning how to learn. With everything earlier mentioned, Chunking refers to organizing or grouping separate pieces of information. When information is 'chunked' into groups, you can remember the information better by remembering the groups as opposed to each part of the information separately.

Most of us can store only about four to seven different items in our short-term memory. One way to get past this limit is to use a technique called Chunking. By grouping several things into one larger whole, you will be able to remember much more. Chunking involves creating something more meaningful—and therefore memorable—from seemingly random bits of information. One example is if you need to place a list of things—such as buying Bananas, Oranges, Apples, and Tamarinds — you can create a word out of the first letters (e.g., "BOAT"), which is easier to remember than the individual items. If you have ever tried to place a phone number by making a word (or words) out of the letters on the phone's dial pad, you have used Chunking.

How to chunk information?

There are several ways to chunk information. Chunking techniques include grouping, finding patterns, and organizing. The method you use to chunk will depend on the information you are chunking. Sometimes more than one course will be possible, but with some practice and insight, it will be possible to determine which technique works best for you.

Chunking as defined by Barbara Oakley: -

Chunking is understanding and practicing with a problem solution so that it can all come to mind in a flash. After you solve a problem, rehearse it. Make sure you can solve it code every step. Pretend it is a song and learn to play it repeatedly in your mind, so the information combines into one smooth chunk you can pull up whenever you want. Many years ago, this process worked for me when I was trying to memorize the nine planets. All I did was simply to use the acronym of the nine to form a different easy sentence. My Very Eye May Just See Under Nine Planets (MVEMJSUNP)! That did the trick!

How to Chunk

- Focus on the information.

- Understand basic/main ideas.

- Practice Chunking Examples

In this chapter, we learn how the use of short codes can help memorize better. The codes are easy to understand, and when we store them in our memory, they allow us access, quite easily, more complex information.

MEMORY

Memories are the internal mental records that we maintain, which give us instant access to our past, complete with all the facts that we know and the skills that we have cultivated. Encoding, storage, and retrieval are the three primary stages of the human memory process.

https://brainworldmagazine.com/learning-memory-how-do-we-remember-and-why-do-we-often-forget/

Our memories have an amazing capability. Albert Einstein once said that we do not even use up to 3% of our memory capacity before we die. Imagine everything we know, imagine how vast these things are; the names of everyone we ever know, the lifelong events, how things happened, dreams we had had several years ago, etc. How we even know people's details once we have met them before and are meeting them again after several years. Despite all of these, we have yet to use 3% of our memory space. What then do you think will be the result if we find a way of using up to 5% of our memory capability?

In this chapter, we understood that our memory capacity is extensive, and even till death, we do not use up to 3% of the space.

ELABORATIVE REHEARSAL

To learn about the process of learning without referring to Elaborate Rehearsal would amount to an absolute waste of time. In learning, elaborate rehearsal is a memory technique that involves thinking about the meaning of the term that needs to learn. It consists of using concepts that are already in your long-term memory to remember ideas that are only in your short-term memory.

When you ruminate over tough topics, and you find yourself relating them with more superficial events, the entire matter becomes a lot easier to learn. Elaborative rehearsal has to do with how well you break the broad subjects down for your understanding.

MAINTENANCE REHEARSAL

Maintenance rehearsal is the technique of repeatedly thinking about or verbalizing a piece of information. It usually works by repetition. Through the consistency of repeating a particular expression, you soon master it.

It works in public life when you surround a child with the things you want him or her to learn; he or she would consistently have these things to think about, and then sooner than later, he or she will understand the things better. Examples of such things in the life of a child are surrounding a child with all the letters of the alphabet; sooner or later; they will be the only thing the child knows.

PASSION

Of all the researchers over the topic of learning psychology, Anthony Angelo had an exciting finding. According to Anthony J.D Angelo, he stated that; "It is essential to develop a passion for learning; if you do, you will never cease to grow." Teachers with passion inspire students; they get a student interested and even excited about what they are learning. Love is what makes students decide to study more. Einstein once said, "Any intelligent fool can make things bigger and more complex. It takes a touch of genius and a lot of courage to move in the opposite direction."

To create passion in studies, the teacher must: -

1. Allocate time for students to do collaborative reviews, even if it is using a social media

2. Foster creativity

3. Allow time to play and have fun with the topic to get them "in the flow to learn."

4. Must keep students interests in mind

5. Inspire more through emotional connections rather than just knowledge

6. And promote innovation.

Passion is the first drive for every learning. If there is no passion for driving the visionary, then it is challenging to accomplish learning. Our passion births every other thing in our academic life. If you are studying a course that you are not passionate about, your results will very likely come out poorly. If you have been failing some courses, you may need to check your passion for those courses. If you find out, however, that passion is lacking, you must start developing a drive toward some of those topics or subjects.

PERSEVERANCE

You have likely heard the word 'Persevere' several times, and I believe you know the essence of it. Its relevance to the subject matter quite well; however, it is essential that we still break down the concept so that you have a broader understanding of how it relates to the subject better. Perseverance originally comes from the Latin word perseverant means to abide by something strictly. Perseverance is not giving up. It is persistence and the effort required to do something and keeps doing it till the end, even if it is hard. Perseverance is persistence in sticking to a plan. An example of determination is working two to three hours each day to study, even if there are no upcoming exams or tests.

Two fundamental belief systems determine how people respond to struggle, setbacks, and failure when pursuing their goals. In one approach, you are likely to get discouraged and give up on your plan. On the other, you tend to embrace the struggle, learn from the setbacks, and keep moving forward – you persevere. Perseverance separates the winners from the losers in both sports and life. Dopamine is the fuel that keeps people motivated to work towards and achieve a goal. You have the power to increase your production of dopamine by changing your attitude and behavior. Scientists have identified higher levels of dopamine — also known as the "reward molecule" — as being linked to forming lifelong habits, such as perseverance.

Tip: -Study in a peaceful ambience. A library is an excellent option if you are accustomed to it. Simply do not go to a room or home after class, instead go to the library, no matter how tired or sleepy you are. Quote - "Most of the critical things in the world have been accomplished by people who had kept on trying when there seemed to be no hope at all." (Dale Carnegie)

Students only persevere in the studies if they find definiteness of purpose in the study; have the desire to learn, self-belief, determination, and a habit to work hard. Perseverance is one of the crucial elements to succeed in difficult times, including learning. An average student tries to avoid or procrastinate instead of persevering on the task. And this essential element is the game-changer in the long run and separates an average performer from a Genius. History has witnessed it again and again.

In this chapter, we learned about how persevering works for a better learning condition. Even the most challenging topics can be understood when we persevere in learning them.

ACTIVE RETRIEVAL

Active retrieval is one of the powerful learning techniques. It involves remembering something that you have learned in the class from your memory. It is an efficient way of moving information from your short-term memory to long term memory so that you can quickly draw it again when you need it. It is always advisable to write down a synopsis or notes that you make after this retrieval. These notes give a snapshot of learning in a flash of seconds. Memos, written down during active retrieval, can be used in making flashcards, one of the oldest techniques in improving learning.

SPACING

Each learning stage creates neural connections. The probability of retaining information quickly or more effectively is through the spacing effect. With spacing or spacing effect, long-term memorization happens. The spacing effect consolidates learned information when the learning events are spaced- out in time. When we space our learning periods, we take the same amount of study time and spread it across a much more extended period. By doing this, the same amount of study time will produce more long-lasting learning.

In summary, if you chock yourself studying without spacing the studies, you may run into a chaotic situation where you will either muddle up everything and give wrong answers to questions.

Space out your studying procedure, interact with the topics, and enjoy the studying process. You will get better rewarded for it in the end. You can even develop reading topics that relate to your current mood. There is always a topic r subject that intrigues your current state.

INTERLEAVING PRACTICE

Not many are familiar with the term 'interleaving practice.' It is, however, strongly related to the topic of learning. Interleaving is a strategy that makes a system more efficient, fast, and reliable by arranging the information in a non-contiguous manner. It allows the information to be retained subconsciously in the brain for the duration and then brings it back to the surface. It contributes to the consolidation of learned info and building better memory connections. Spaced learning and interleaving practice are the best strategies that complement each other while boosting better learning. These two techniques can be changed or used interchangeably to promote better consolidation of information.

NAPPING BETWEEN STUDIES

Naps can increase alertness during the period immediately after the rest, and this can be used to improve learning. A small nap just after a study helps the brain in consolidating learned information and can transfer it to the long-term memory quickly. Nap duration can vary from 45 minutes to 90 minutes, depending on the person and their ability to relax at will.

• Even for well-rested people, naps can improve performance in areas such as reaction time, logical reasoning, and symbol recognition, as Cote described in a 2009 review (Journal of Sleep Research, 2009). They can also be useful for one's mood.

- A study by University of Michigan doctoral student Jennifer Goldschmied and colleagues found that after waking from a 60-minute midday nap, people were less impulsive and had a greater tolerance for frustration than people who watched an hour-long nature documentary instead of sleeping (Personality and Individual Differences, 2015). "Frustration tolerance is one facet of emotion regulation," says Goldschmied. "

- "What's amazing is that in a 90-minute nap, you can get the same [learning] benefits as an eight-hour sleep period," Mednick says. "And actually, the nap is having an additive benefit on top of a good night of sleep."

- In another experiment, Mednick found that an afternoon nap was about equal to a dose of caffeine for improving perceptual learning. But in other ways, a midday doze might trump your afternoon latte. She found people who napped performed better on a verbal word-recall task an hour after waking compared with people who took caffeine or a placebo (Behavioural Brain Research, 2008). While caffeine enhances alertness and attention, naps boost those abilities in addition to improving some forms of memory consolidation, Mednick notes.

• Other research builds the case that the hippocampus benefits from a nap. Matthew Walker, Ph.D., a professor of psychology at the University of California, Berkeley, and colleagues recruited volunteers to tax their associative memories by learning a long list of name-face pairings.

• Half the participants then took 90-minute midday naps. That evening, the participants were given a new round of learning exercises with novel pairings. Those who had not napped did not perform as well on the evening test as they had in the morning. But the nappers did better on the later test, suggesting the sleep had boosted their capacity for Learning (Current Biology, 2011).

• According to new research, all we would need is a solid 10-minute power nap to boost our focus and productivity. Researchers tested four nap periods: 5, 10, 20, and 30 minutes (and a control group that did not nap). They then tested participants across several benefits for three hours after the nap. Here is a summary of the results: The 5-minute nap produced few benefits in comparison with the no-nap control. The 10-minute nap made immediate improvements in all outcome measures (including sleep latency, subjective sleepiness, fatigue, vigour, and cognitive performance), with some of these benefits maintained for as long as 155 minutes. The "20-minute nap" was associated with improvements lasting up to 125 minutes after napping. The 30-minute nap produced a period of impaired alertness and performance immediately after napping, indicative of sleep inertia, followed by improvements lasting up to 155 minutes after the rest.

References: - http://www.apa.org/monitor/2016/07-08/naps.aspx

In summary, Napping is essential for effective learning. It helps the reader assimilate better, and it increases the longevity of the learned lessons in-memory storage.

COOPERATIVE LEARNING

Cooperative Learning is the process of breaking a classroom of students into small groups so that they can discover a new concept together and help each other learn. An example of cooperative Learning is a teacher asking students to analyze a tree, and each student is required to research one component like leaves, root, bark, and stem and then teach it to the other students. It provides an optimum challenge and generates interest, and everyone tries to do their best. The purpose of cooperative learning groups is to make each member a healthier individual in his or her right. Students learn together so that they can subsequently perform higher as individuals. The essential element of cooperative learning is teaching students the required interpersonal and small group skills.

In general, cooperative learning raises the achievements of students, builds a positive relationship with peers, creates a learning community that values diversity, and promotes good knowledge and social skills.

Types of Cooperative Learning

Formal Cooperative Learning

Formal cooperative learning consists of students working together, for one class period to several weeks, to achieve shared learning goals and complete jointly specific tasks and assignments (Johnson, Johnson, & Holubec, 2008).

Informal Cooperative Learning

Informal cooperative Learning consists of having students work together to achieve a joint learning goal is temporary, ad-hoc groups that last from a few minutes to one class period (Johnson, Johnson, & Holubec, 2008).

Cooperative Base Groups

Cooperative base groups are long-term, heterogeneous collaborative learning groups with stable membership (Johnson, Johnson, & Holubec, 2008). Members' primary responsibilities are to-

(a) Ensure all members are making satisfactory academic progress (i.e., positive goal interdependence)

(b) Hold each other accountable for striving to learn (i.e., individual accountability), and

(c) Provide each other with support, encouragement, and assistance in completing assignments (i.e., promotive interaction).

In the above narration, we have learned that breaking into smaller learning units will enable students to understand a topic better. When mates discuss the topics, they can give an account of the topic better.

DEBATE

The debate, as a teaching tool, can be traced back to ancient Greece. Debating is a method of discussion and analyzing issues. Debaters aimed to persuade others to accept or believe their arguments on a topic. For a debate, you need a case, a debating team (an affirmative team and opposing team), a team structure, team line, matter, method, manner, rebuttal, and an adjudicator.

A debate allows students to explore and gain an understanding of alternative viewpoints, develops communication & critical thinking and argumentation skills necessary for the development of a knowledge base.

A Quote from a study, "The debate is a method of formally presenting an argument in a structured manner. Through logical consistency, factual accuracy, and some degree of emotional appeal to the audience are elements in debating, where one side often prevails over the other party by presenting a superior "context" and framework of the issue. The outcome of a debate may depend upon consensus or some formal way of resolving, rather than the objective facts." In a traditional debating contest, there are rules for participants to discuss and decide on differences within a framework defining how they will interact.

Teachers often use the debate to effectively increase student's involvement and participation during tutorial/seminar sessions, especially within the Humanities and Social Sciences and within some selective Science courses. When a teacher uses the debate as a framework for learning, s/he hopes to get students to conduct comprehensive research into the topic, gather supporting evidence, engage in collaborative learning, delegate tasks, improve communication skills, and develop leadership and team-skills - all at one go.

Quote from the website - "Decades of academic research have proven that the benefits that accrue because of engaging in the debate are numerous. Debate provides experiences that are conducive to life-changing, cognitive, and presentational skills.". Also, through discussion, debaters acquire unique educational benefits as they learn and polish skills, far beyond what can be learned in any other setting.

Debating has the following benefits: -

- Debaters become better critical thinkers and communicators. People begin to see them differently.

- Debaters improve their social interactions and are not argumentative with their family and friends, but oddly enough, more understanding.
- Debaters improve their expression & their voices are listened to.
- Debaters are frequently identified as leaders in practice. "Studies in America show that those who communicate often and well, and give a balance of positive and negative comments, are leaders."
- "Debaters tend to become citizens in the real sense of the word — informed, active, participating, a force to be harnessed for the betterment of all."
- N.B.: - Children who are good at constructive debates have a higher potential to reach their goals.

In summary, debating widens a student's understanding of a topic. If the student can debate over the subject effectively, it gives the student an opportunity of identifying spots he had not initially seen.

DISCUSSION

Discussion is essential to learning because it helps students process information rather than merely receiving it. The goal of a discussion is to get students to practice thinking about the course material, and that makes the role of a teacher as a facilitator. Open-ended discussion promotes a collaborative exchange of ideas among a teacher and students. It encourages students thinking, learning, problem-solving, understanding or appreciation of learning Discussion-based teaching help learner in the acquisition of knowledge, skills, and attitudes through discourse rather than passive approaches that focus on lecture reading or viewing. It promotes learning both for teachers and students.

Discussion-based learning increases students' interest, and engagement in the topic and helps them to maintain focus. When asked to clarify their views, students understand different perspectives on the subject. Right questions and answers can get their students to think deeply and make better neuronal connections in the brain.

Just as we have identified in the previous chapters, students learn better when they orally express their opinions over a topic. Discussion facilitates the learning process; oral discussion helps boost retention.

DRAMATIC PLAY

Dramatic play is a type of game "where children accept and assign roles, and then act them out.".

Quote – "It is a time when they break through the walls of reality, pretend to be someone or something different from themselves, and dramatize situations and actions to go along with the roles they have chosen to play. And while this type of play may be viewed as frivolous by some, it remains an integral part of the developmental learning process by allowing children to develop skills in such areas as abstract thinking, literacy, math, and social studies in a timely, natural manner."

TYPES OF PLAY

There are two types of play, which is structured and unstructured play:

• Structured play has a predetermined set and desired outcome. A parent or teacher sets up a scenario for the children to play into, such as setting up a "Market," and the children then choose and assign roles from what is available. Structured play helps children in integrating a focused mode of thinking. It helps them to learn problem-solving and collective decision making.

• Unstructured play is where children have the freedom to choose their plan scenarios and often create their own sets based on what is available to them. This play helps children to explore their inner subconscious brain and promotes a diffused mode of thinking and problem-solving. It also brings out the creativity of the child to the surface.

Benefits of Dramatic Play: -

1. Dramatic play teaches self-regulation

2. Encourages language development

3. Teaches conflict resolution

4. Supports literacy

5. Relieves emotional tension and is empowering to children

Children good in acting out or mimicry are potentially smarter & mature than their peers.

Conclusively, students are intrigued when they see or act in the drama. While learning, dramatizing or allowing the learners some room to dramatize their new knowledge helps them understand better.

EXPERIMENTAL LEARNING

Experiential learning is one of the most effective styles or strategies in teaching. This type of education helps the learner to be purposefully engaged with the understanding, develop new skills, clarify misconceptions, and develop the student's capacity to experiment.

Four models are available under the Process of Experiential Learning: -

1. Lewinian developed a model used in lab research and training.

2. Dewey's model of Learning

3. Piaget's model of learning and cognitive development

4. Kolb's an experiential learning model

Hands-on learning is a form of experiential learning but does not involve a student's reflection on teaching.

Main benefits of experiential learning: -

A. The learning process educates learners on the competencies they should have for life success.

B. It drives the students to achieve aims.

C. Students learn how to guide themselves properly through the learning process.

Summarily, students understand how the lessons taught work in real-life circumstances, Experimental learning provides motivation for the students, and it gives them a better idea of the subject. It even offers insights to the students.

INSTRUCTIONAL EFFECTIVENESS

World-famous Educationalist & Mathematician Anant Kumar (Owner of Super 30) says, "Hard work, Proper guidance and Supervision are the secrets of success" in students' learning. Anant's simple speech is entirely relevant to our teenager's learning strategies today. He has shown his opinion beyond any reasonable doubt, and hence it is essential to focus on Instructional effectiveness, which includes both Guidance & Supervision in Learning.

We can discuss a lot about the role of the Teacher, Quality of Teaching, Impact of practical teaching on the student's achievement. "But it cannot be denied that it is the teacher who lays the foundation of good learning." On a general note, the teachers or lecturers can positively develop or demotivate the learners from a particular subject.

For students to learn effectively, the following must be in place: -

1. Educator must create an interest in the topic.

2. How optimistic is the instructor in the applied scope of the issue?

3. How is the topic introduced to students?

4. How does the instructor respond to the queries?

5. Finally, how is the effort on the part of the student rewarded? Keeping track of all these critical points may be difficult for some instructors, which leads to variation in the learning of different students in different places.

LECTURE METHOD

The word 'lecture' originates from Latin. It was originally a Latin term, from as far back as the 14th and 15th century, 'Lecture' translates roughly into "the act of reading." The first time the word was used to indicate verbal lectures was in the 16th century. It was then used to depict the act of a lecturer standing in front of the students to impart knowledge.

In recent times, the term now implies that teaching method involving first and foremost, a vocal performance given by a teacher to a group of scholars. Many addresses are conveyed by some sort of pictorial aid, for example, slideshows, word text, an image, or a picture. Teachers may even use a whiteboard, chalkboard to emphasize essential points in their lecture, but a class does not require any of these things to qualify as a lecture. An influential person at the front of a class or gathering, delivering an educative discourse to a group of listeners, this can be called a lecture."

Advantages of Lecture method as one of learning strategy: -

1. Teacher control

2. New material

3. Effortless

Disadvantages: -

1. One way

2. Passive

3. Strong expectations from the speaker

The lecturer must inculcate interest in the subject. This interest must lead the audience to explore the topic on his/her own. Learning is facilitated based on the curiosity that a lecturer creates in the students to explore the subject. It also means that, if the lecturer is passive in their approach, a student will not develop an interest in the matter.

PEER TEACHING

Peer teaching is one of the best methods of learning. It is the one which I like the most. When you are speaking to your peers about the subject, you do it at a sub bar conscious level. It makes the topic register itself in long-term memory, especially for those who are auditory learners.

Students not only find it amusing or exciting to hear their peers act as the teachers; they also learn better under such conditions. The eagerness to teach their peers too thrills the students. In the end, peer teaching is of considerable advantage to the entire learning process.

ROLE-PLAYING

Learning is at best when we can enact the teaching to our audience in a way that can make them understand it. Role-playing involves a deep understanding of the subject.

Role-playing encourages the creativity and imagination of students as it allows them to make mistakes in a non-threatening environment. It also helps them to develop social and emotional skills in addition to physical development. And the process of role-playing involves enhancing communication skills in addition to enriching their language skills. Like dramatizing, the students are given roles to play as part of the teaching process. Picking up positions help the students associate the topics or subject to faces. We learn faster when we associate looks to topics.

PEG WORD MNEMONICS

A mnemonic is a strategy to help in retaining important information for the future. It is a form of associated learning where a person must enlist the information in such a way that it can make a rhythm that is easy to remember.

Mnemonics can be in the form of Music, Rhyme, Image, Connection, Word, or Name.

For example, as I earlier said too, this is one of the Mnemonic that can be used to remember the planets. Men Vary Every Moment Just Singing Under New Platform.

When words are pegged in that manner, remaining only a fraction will help you remember a vast proportion of the teaching. It is like coding the phrase.

SLEEP

Sleep is not only a state of unconsciousness but a naturally recurring mind activity of the body. Sleep is essential for humans to remain sane. Just like food, sleep is equally necessary for our survival. If we do not sleep well, all human beings will behave just like robots. Human beings need the right sleeping protocol for the better functioning of our grey matter. Scientists have revealed that improper sleep can be the cause of any of the following conditions: -

1. Alzheimer's (after a long time)

2. Lack of attention and concentration

3. Anxiety

4. Depression

5. Chronic pain(s)

Conditions necessary for a good sleep routine: -

1. A cooler dark room with a temperature lower than the optimum room temperature in your living room.

2.. Avoid taking beverages like tea and especially coffee because of caffeine.

3. Do not eat fatty food like cheese etc.

4.Not to keep media gadget in the vicinity of your bedroom

Note: -Those who sleep better, learn better

NOTES TAKING METHOD

After the completion of a fair reading process or during a lecture session, it is indispensable to jot down notes, most notably in your terms of understanding (i.e., in a way you would understand). Students must ensure that they take notes that are relevant to the topic learned. Note-taking pattern emulated must be compatible with their style of learning.

While learning, teenagers and youth generally have a great tendency to feel that they would always remember the experience of learning. The memory is the greatest deceiver, however, because as soon as the lectures are over, the things assumed learned still fly out of their memory capacity. Notes taken during the class in own handwriting makes it easier for the student to retrieve the learning material. When we go over our notes, we recall all the things that we are told and discussed on the day.

MEMORY BOOSTING TECHNIQUES

Researchers who have worked on teenage learning strategies have found that it is possible to improve memory by using methods that engage certain parts of the brain, also known as brain plasticity. The best example of the strategies is the recovery that has been trained following CVA/stroke. The aim of the therapist in this recovery process is aimed at retraining certain parts of the brain to take over the lost functions from the other parts after the infliction of an injury. Some of the results of the test are awesome; for instance, it takes a little close to two hundred repeatedly affected limbs to index an engram that has everything to do with that movement in the brain.

There are various memory boosting methods. Teenagers can access a great lot when they surf online, but it is healthier to read books at libraries where they can more seriously get compendiums of needed information.

GRIT

Quote from the study:- "When we talk about Grit, under teenage learning strategies, we are talking about a non-cognitive factor which has, among other things, received increased attention lately, researchers have pointed out the fact that it plays a significant role in successful outcomes in various fields, and more specifically in teenage learning and general education." Grit has its roots in two facets; the facets include consistency in the topic of interest and effort perseverance, taken by the Grit Scale. The present logical review aimed at examining the association of grit with positive enlightening outcomes by exploring both backgrounds and outcomes. Grit is related to retaining and routine in the soldierly, the work, and the institute. In the school context, grit has been associated with pointers of institutional achievements, such as students' CGPA in schools and colleges. Quote-"For many years now, the distinctions of grit in academic success have been tested due to only low-to-moderate associations between these two constructs, as well as grit's low growing validity above and beyond meticulousness and self-regulation." A possible elucidation of these findings shows that a lot of extant research has engaged an overall sum score of grit by combining two facet-level scores. When grit was inspected as having separate duo dimensions, PE displayed stronger associations with theoretical accomplishment than overall grit scores (also known as CI). In answer to former restrictions, this study hypothesized grit as two-faced perspectives to better reveal the associations between grit and academic outcomes.

Scientific research and findings have been checked to examine Grit in an education. The primary result of the works carried out revealed that grit shows weak to moderate associations with instructive variables. The two aspects purpose differently, with the determination being a tougher positive forecaster of academic performance. In the case of positive variables, (an example of this is hope). It positively affects family relationships, and it can increase grit. A deeper understanding of the grit construct is important to differentiate it from facets of the thoroughness dimension of disposition. The practicality of findings for policymakers and education professionals is deliberated, as well as the importance of buttressing grit in the enlightening community to cultivate character in students and augment their potential.

Among various learning stations, Academic knowledge is an incremental procedure that requires determination of effort, particularly in the face of challenges and hindrances. Recent research has shown that grit, defined as desire and determination in the quest for long-term goals, is a key factor related to student engagement and academic achievement. It implies that students who work hard but also love "what they do" are likely to accomplish better. The hypothesis of grit describes it as "a resource of mental strength, which is unique and essential to some cultures, especially the Finnish culture and the collective academic dissertation." In different languages, there are ways in which they describe grit; the Finnish word is 'Sisu,' which is often rendered as grit. It denotes a determination to overcome adversity and is alleged by Finns as a trademark of their national personality. With Grit, Finnish people subsisted through the harsh, cold winter and offences of the Soviet Union and became one of the most technically progressive and happiest republics in the world. Despite the prominent role of grit in academic learning in general and in Finnish culture specifically, few empirical studies using a longitudinal study design have scrutinized the factors that promote grit among teenagers and precisely in the Finnish school setting. As such, this study concentration is based on two theoretically driven mental forerunners, examining whether teenagers who have a growth mindset and high obligation to their educational objectives tend to be gritty in educational learning.

In a research result, the impact of grit on achievement was smaller than the effect of expectancies of success, ability, self-concept, or school engagement. However, determination had an immediate consequence as with those of self-efficacy and other similar traits.

EXPLICIT REMEMBERING

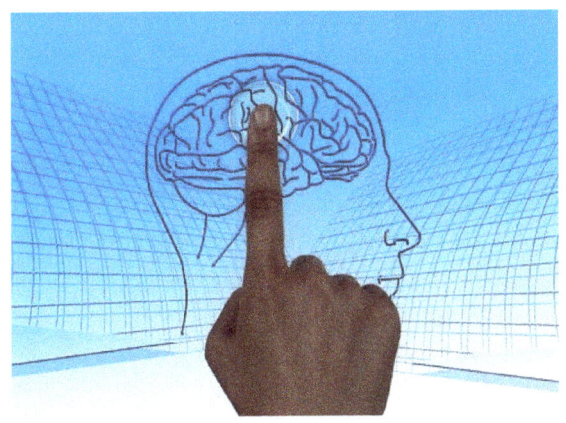

Students that would learn must always train themselves on how well they remember things; between Implicit and Explicit memory, explicit memory is the most effective. It refers to conscious memories that we can intentionally recall and articulate. It can be divided into those that involve remembering or recalling personal experiences and those that include memorizing facts (data) and information.

Implicit reminiscences are much faster to acquire or retain than vivid reminiscences. Implicit memories can be remembered for a long time even by a single stimulus, whereas the formation of an explicit memory always requires multiple rounds of stimulation and reaction. That is why a teenage learner cannot immediately memorize an entire page in a book after glancing through it once. There is a hippocampus that is found deep in the brain; it is within the temporal lobe of the brain. The hippocampus's function is particularly essential for consolidating data from a short term to long-term memory, as well as latitudinal cognizance. The prefrontal cortex is compulsory for the storage and reclamation of long-term remembrances, chiefly facts, and information. Meanwhile, there is also an amygdala, which is a small structure that is located near the hippocampus. The function has to do with emotional memory and observation.

In the following paragraphs, we shall look at some examples.

1. Self-composed memories have to do with how we build a more general picture of the events all through our life. These are a combination of semantic memories and episodic

reminiscences. For example, unless the event was recorded, you cannot practically remember being born, but you are told, and so you know the city in which you were born.

2. Longitudinal memories are how we circumnavigate the world around us, and this is the reason we can easily find our way around acquainted towns.

3. Declarative memory (also called "Clearly-Displayed") is one out of the two major subdivisions of long-term memory. (The other subdivision is implicit memory.) Explicit memory has to do with conscious thought—such as recalling who came to dinner last night or giving the names of animals that live in the rainforest. It is what most people define within them as the definition of "memory," It can be called a lay man's mere understanding of memory. It also has to do with whether it is good or bad. This memory is usually associative; the brain connects memories. Let's examine the following illustration; when you think of a word or occasion, such as a vehicle, your retention can bring up a whole host of

associated recollections—from carburettors to your shuttle to a family road trip to a hundred other things.

4. Sequence memories are our personal experiences, such as the ability to recall events that occurred throughout our lives.

5. Semantic memories are the remembrance of pieces of data, descriptions, and notions. For example, recalling the key events of the American Political Wars or being able to remember how digestion works in people.

INTERESTING APPLICATION OF LEARNING

Learning is an exciting venture; after pictorial depiction, it is the best receptive method. However, quite a lot of people have challenges in being able to comprehend the information being listened to entirely. The various application of learning to know involves the following categories.

Casting

Casting or role-playing is also another practical approach founded on active learning methods. Role-playing feigns real-life circumstances that require problem-solving abilities. More importantly, it is also a medium for assessing actual performance. Role-playing activities can include job replications like customer relations (facilitator plays the customer and the learner play the agent or vice versa) through the phones, social media, email, chats, or in some cases, virtual reality.

Deep Reflection

These two are methods can also be categorized under active education methods. Imitating is staple method for any problem-solving action. These sessions have to do with learners coming up with ideas and posting them on the board. As a group, the students then pick the best ones and make use of those chosen to come up with a clarification. For methods like these, there are available applications that allow learners to use personally owned devices to collaborate with others in coming up with a map tree, an idea, or a concept.

Hunting

Hunting (or fishing) is another entertaining and appealing doing that involves the use of the company information base. Hunting starts with a client's concern. The learner's task is to use the scheme to find the perfect resource to attend to the issue. Not only does it get the learners familiar with the system, but it also prepares them to handle real-life customer circumstances.

Joint Virtual Classrooms

Collaborative cybernetic classrooms make connected learning more engaging. Aside from the usual audio-video conferencing and tête-à-tête structures, virtual classrooms also deliver synchronous and asynchronous explanation, messages, and resource sharing for organizers and partakers. It is a particular condition for any eLearning policy.

Most of the teenage students who graduate from secondary schools are not interested in pursuing professions in scholarship related fields. The most common reason given for that is they never enjoyed studying the subjects. Factors can be many like a method of teaching, disposition of teacher, not enough interest generated in the matter, or students not finding any interesting in the application of the subject. The methods employed for learning limits on how many students will understand the topic or subject. Motivating methods can be gotten from reading books such as this or through making research to discover better strategies.

Tools for Raw Fact or Solution Providers

A blend of a searcher hunt and role-playing activity, this exercise is one of the more effective active learning stratagems for grownups. The organizer assigns a case-study (if possible, taken from everyday customer situations) to an apprentice. The learner then makes sense of the information and uses the available means to solve the case.

Social Media Messages

Social media or online discussion boards are also one of many proven active involvement stratagems. Social Media channels are virtual boards where students can learn jointly. They post inquiries and answer queries. Most of the time, there is a minimal organizer or focus matter expert intercession involved, with most answers usually coming from the other contributors who are more well-informed on the topic.

Exemplary Learning

Exemplary Leaning suggests that you consent learners to prepare and teach the lessons (or just a fraction of them) to their fellow learners. Although it may look like the facilitator is taking a very hands-off approach in this method, because one would expect the facilitator to be in full control of the activity, it involves a very elaborate process where the teacher is both moderator and coordinator and expert.

Ensure that you note that learning by teaching does not merely mean a presentation or a lecture accessible by the learners. In this specific approach, teenage students are the ones who are expediting the session by engaging with fellow pupils. The facilitator ensures that the learning gets administered correctly and lends a hand to the student-hosts after observing their flops. Webinars and online discussion boards are the standard media used for this approach.

Riddle System

Riddle System is another line that fully reaps the benefits of active participation and shares learning. In this approach, students are given a "piece of the riddle" that they need to solve on their own. After this, they need to collaborate with other learners to complete the riddle finally.

The riddle system is a perfect addition to role-playing, and it involves using information or apparatuses to solve what might seem like more significant problems and give participants a glimpse of the 'better image.' It is a worthy exercise to let learners realize their role in the better image by doing both individual and collaborative work and how those are all part of a procedure.

Although a few have been mentioned above, there are still multitudes of activities for active learning methods out there. With the help of advanced equipment, learning managers and professionals have been presented more options on how to engage today's tech-dependent spectators better. However, it will now be a matter of time before technology improves again and learning policies progresses with it. Learning professionals just must keep up and familiarize themselves with the system if they do not want to get disconnected from their learners. Whatever method works for any teacher is best to be engaged in the learning process. The approach adopted must be critically examined.

In conclusion, students must apply interesting methods to the adopted learning process.

LOW STAKE QUIZZING

There are countless advantages in employing Low Stake Quizzing. While learning how to learn, we shall only refer to a few:

1. Provides learners with multiple opportunities to demonstrate understanding.

2. Encourages learners to take ownership of their learning.

3. Allows for instructors to direct learners to the proper resources to fill potential learning gaps.

4. Encourages interaction with the learning content.

5. Encourages learners to achieve mastery.

6. Reduces learner anxiety often associated with online quizzes and exams.

7. Allows learners to identify and self-remedy potential learning gaps.

There are a lot more. It is recommended, however, that meaningful feedback be comprised of the following elements: Reference to find the answer and additional resources on the topic, Statement of the correct answer, Detailed explanation of the solution.

Inclusion of these rudiments encourages the learner to not only garner an explanation of the precise answer but also to interact with the content filling any learning gaps that may happen on their own. Furthermore, since multiple attempts have been allowed, the student may return to the assessment, further inspiring mastery.

Low stakes testing with meaningful response does not punish pupils for making mistakes, but in its place, shifts the focus to broader understanding or professionalism. It encourages the learner to try, and if an error is made, it may be provided with meaningful direction on how to correct the mistake when no one else is there.

The idea of the test being 'low stakes' is essential. In practical testing, it is not expected to, or it should not be a pass or fail assessment check. It should avoid creating unnecessary anxiety and stress for the tender teenage learner.

Low stakes testing is an excellent way of getting pupils to retrieve facts and track whether pupils remember critical aspects of the topic taught. Having an organized (written down) list of knowledge is your primary point, such as Average Term Plans/Schemes of Learning.

Running topic-based assessments (rather than a mix of retrieval topics) can give good comprehension into pupil/class strengths and areas for expansion. Although inserting is an important aspect of current discerning in terms of education, mixing up the actual valuation can lead to misperception, especially if knowledge is assessed within topic-based classifications.

SPACING OUT PRACTICE

One of the most vital aspects of learning how to learn is to know how to engage the spacing out practice. What does that mean? You would ask. There is substantial evidence that spaced way, dispersed practice, or spread-out repetition outperforms massed learning or "fill up" strategies. Multiple mental functions are responsible for the advantageous effects of spread-out practice. The most prevalent of these are procedural learning, readying outcomes, and growing retrieval.

Some policies must be applied in spacing out for significant achievement. The process can be extended depending on individuals.

Enjoy engaging it in — one easy betting tactic that has been popularly employed in new technical means can be modified for spaced practice. Mix "Woman Crush Wednesday" or "Thank God It's Friday" to help keep a broader array of content in play with pupils at any point in time.

Dividing the steps; by breaking the steps into more manageable stages, it will be able to follow up. Presentation of students who hear content one time, in one discourse, will be lower than those who regularly revisit content.

Use Effective Slide Apps: Design education resources that are less focused around a singular PowerPoint address topic. Generate opportunities for "useful distress" in a safe learning situation to help schoolchildren —and yourself—understand where knowledge gaps are. Make sure beginners are involved too. Model spaced repetition by outlining and showcasing your spread-out practice strategies for the session.

Call the Consideration of pupils that spaced practice will feel more challenging in the beginning and make them question their obliviousness in general. Repeat it in the ears of the students that worthy time education must be part of the equality in space tryout. Spaced practice can also take different forms, such as using some apps drawing relationships on whiteboards, simulation, and anatomy labs, as well as the library or local coffee shop.

Encourage your pupils to organize a study plan that reserves to them more sections, or fractions of their time, over the block, session, or year. Anticipate that cramming or stuffing all in their brains all at once will be a difficult habit to break, especially when the benefits of sustained learning are often not fully apparent until weeks, months, and years later. Eventually, scheduled spaced practice over time will produce desirable results that the student should notice going into high stakes situations.

Avoid refusing to engage in technological aids. Make learning tips and resources a regular part of your Picture template. Especially when you need to drive learning toward schoolchildren in a prearranged structure and short timeframe, make sure you use modern applications that can make it a whole lot easier for you.

POSITIVITY IN THE SURROUNDING

While learning to learn, it is essential to reiterate that the learning environment plays a vital role in the assessment of the students learning capability. The gathering environment plays a crucial role in children's academic output. A positive environment releases a positive vibe to make the students eager or yearn for the topic. In such an atmosphere, the students feel that strong sense of readiness to learn, they develop trust for their teacher and mates, they are eager to tackle questions, and the desire to be part of the learning even more.

Many people are familiar with all the factors that can threaten a positive classroom environment: problems that kids bring from home, lack of inspiration among students whose love of education has been pierced right out of them, burdens from testing, and more. We cannot control all these factors, but what if we could device some simple approaches to cushion their negative effects? What if we could create the right solutions?

On the optimistic side, we can continuously adapt effective learning and, by that, transform the experience of our students every day. This can be achieved by harnessing the power of mental or emotional engagement. If you are already objecting that you do not have the luxury of time for that kind of activity, then do not bother about engaging in it at all. This is not implying that you should stop holding a daily class meeting that would help talk about feelings. The strategies that have been offered in this book can be easily integrated into everyday teaching. These teachings are not a huge threat or a frill. You can ignore the power of mental engagement at the teacher's risk. When we dismiss the negative or positive effects, when we disregard the fact that emotions have a significant impact on learning, we make our jobs more challenging for us and others. Plentiful research summarizes the impact feelings have on education. Strain or pressure, for example, has unfair results on student's cognitive functioning. Regrettably, when it comes to knowledge procedures, the power of undesirable events greatly overshadows the ability of progressive events. As a result, we need to arm ourselves with an arsenal of strategies that immunizes our students against the power of unhelpfulness. Sufficient provision of progressive experiences must be available to counter the destructive. These simple procedures help students evade getting caught in an adverse spiral, which can be set off by something as harmless as a critical reference from a mate or a stressful assessment instant. Being caught up in negative sentiments in such a manner disturbs learning by narrowing students' focus and constraining their ability to see multiple belvederes to create solutions to or solve problems that can be challenging.

Frankly, the aim of this book is not to serve as a short-cut provider, and there is no shortcut, there is no Band-Aid either, that will fix that distressed kid and send him to a magical haven of learning. Instead, it is a conductor to guileless procedures, strategies, and constructions that take little time to the device yet yield lasting results. Creating a positive environment produces a powerful undulating effect that continually enhances learning: when scholars can see the comicality in their errors, rejoice at their successes, and feel authorized as change agents, they will actively engage in learning and, consequently, learn more efficiently. Far from capable, straightforward clarifications and instant results, these strategies will increase students' capacity to bear the uneasiness that comes with working hard besides to accept that there are no easy responses—that only critical, intelligent discernment and perseverance lead the way to excellent knowledge.

Some methods will help you evaluate the challenges you face in the classroom and discourse them by infusing your practice with progressive elements like hilarity, novelty, and interest. The first step is to examine the current state of your educational setting and check the proportion of the effectiveness and how it has been to you so far. If you find yourself wanting, then you should identify areas you need to improve and consequently improve on them.

REFLECTION

What is reflection? And what is its relevance to teenage learning?

Reflection is built on the concept of thoughtful learning. This theory underscores that understanding arises from our experiences and can be regularly modernized through the process of recording and thinking about the experiences we have. A very vital aspect of thoughtful learning is that it is a progression in which we can learn about ourselves. One of the most noticeable examiners of the topic - Malcolm Gibbs' in his findings discovered some stages of reflection which help students to make sense of their knowledge experiences. In higher education and graduate service, high value is placed on the skill of being a thoughtful learner. The direct insinuation of this extends from making themselves more independent learners to evaluate their learning merely critically to classifying areas of their knowledge that require further development.

The next question about the relevance of the topic to the subject matter will be to think about ways in which everyone can develop his practice in relationship with the bearing. We all imitate naturally from time to time, things that happen to us, i.e., our experiences. Reflection makes this process more official. Often, scholars are required to write their thoughts in the form of a blog or insightful statement. This encourages a habit in scholars, which is deemed to be useful in becoming a more philosophical learner.

A vital beginning stage for consideration is to recognize a severe event; this was the observation of Brookfield in a 1987 publication. It does not have to be a theatrical occasion; it only must have caused a sequence of opinions, which results in the students learning something new about one another.

Of the prominence of this idea, some remarkable fields show the reflective attributes. Some of the areas are Reflective learning and writing study guide, how your reflective writing will be marked, Characteristics of reflective and academic essay, and Double-entry journal.

Advantages of Reflection

1. Reflection develops your self-awareness
2. Reflection makes you know your strengths and weaknesses
3. It helps you learn from your mistakes
4. Reflection enables you to understand how you learn
5. Reflection helps record your development
6. It helps plan your development
7. It allows you to learn about yourself
8. Articulate your skills/learning to others

9. Reflection provides more information

Some of the useful areas of reflecting involves, ability to ask questions to provoke thought, defining the term Reflection, structuring writing reflectively

SPACE VISUALIZATION

For those who do not know before now, Space Visualization, also known as spatial imaging, is what adopts the double dimensional instructions and translates them into a trio dimensional object that one is making efforts to build. With all said so far, Space Visualization is essential. Learning involves our ability to comprehend visually. Everyone has his or her unique strengths. Some people are gifted athletes, while others can deliver motivational speeches or sight-read music. It is not hard to identify a few people who can navigate through a forest, even without the use of a map. Some others can even draw unique paintings or even draw people in their exact likenesses. You may be an expert at algebra, trigonometry, or at comforting your friends in a manner that they end up feeling exceedingly relieved.

Anthony Marcus, a developmental psychologist, referred to these strengths as brilliant traits. Marcus concluded after observing that the ways that people reason and relate with one another could be divided into ten authorized classes. These classes range from musical ability to rational ability to three-dimensional skill, and they comprise most of the capacities that people possess. Some of these abilities are easy to comprehend. If someone is expressly capable of dancing exceptionally, it is a reasonable expectation that such person has bodily kinesthetic astuteness. The same goes for musical understanding. It is not difficult to match a good voice or to play a musical instrument with this category of abilities.

However, some other people, they find it more difficult to distinguish. For example, visual-spatial intelligence regularly obscures the public with its seeming wideness. That said, like the other intelligence proposed by Marcus, visual-spatial acumen explains a variety of conversational abilities. One of these is spatial imagining.

Although, the subject may sometimes be confusing, especially if one compares it to the ease of matching the harmonious ability to melodious astuteness.

What exactly is spatial visualization?

Spatial imagining is the gift to ponder in three-dimensions and, more specifically, to maneuver just a pair and then trio dimensional objects mentally. A variety of professions use it to achieve more significant results in their engagements, but it is also necessary for everyday life. Nowadays, there is hardly anyone who does not use spatial visualization daily; some professions give more priority to this ability.

When creating art, artists use spatial visualization to determine how trio-dimensional kinds of stuff should look next to one other. They also decide the size of an object, what that object looks like when viewing from a different point of view, and what size it takes when compared to the other things around. This all draws on spatial visualization skills. Other fields that use spatial visualization in their everyday activities are photographers, graphic designers, painters, architects, musicians, geologists, decorators, and surgeons. Even engineers are one of the most notable examples of professionals who engage in spatial visualization in their daily engagement. Their duty requires activities that need to be broken down into a whole host of other sub-disciplines. Though, being an engineer is, at its core, about scheming, evolving, and cultivating some invention. Civil engineers might design underpasses or channels, while automatic engineers develop apparatuses and machines. Those in the engineering field must think about ways of converting their double dimensional works to make it three dimensional. The concerned topic is quite relevant to achieve this.

Although spatial imagining is often paired with knowledge and calculation, other professions also use spatial visualization. For instance, performers, painters, and graphic designers use the same spatial imagining skills that engineers use. Some colleges even necessitate scholars to take spatial visualization tests and examinations before enrolling in a manufacturing program. Likewise, many engineering programs include sessions that help students improve their spatial visualization services. Many of us, for example, have acquired equipment that is flat pack. It may be available in a package and left for the consumer or buyer to assemble; this flat-pack equipment frequently comes with picture-heavy guidelines to help the buyer build his or her brand new piece of equipment. Constructing your equipment may seem complicated. But, aside from those tiny, easy-to-lose struggles, the only tool you need to prosper is spatial visualization. Simply putting what looks like into what it fits into gets it done easy!

Much like putting together fittings in a house, many activities that involve following directions require spatial visualization. For instance, making use of a map is a spatial activity. You must observe the plan critically to decide how that dimensional duo picture applies to your physical environment.

Stitching something from a pattern also uses this skill. To sew a blouse, you must observe an initial design of that clothing item and reflect on how to bring that intention to life. Especially making the garment the perfect fitting requires a good spatial visualization gift.

The same goes for organizing groceries in a car's trunk, packing a suitcase, or putting things away in a briefcase or travel bag. Spatial visualization enables us to envision in our thoughts and then actualize the best way of creating these items.

How Do We Get Access to Spatial Visualization?

Since visualization, as we have now seen it, is essential in the workplace and the larger world, psychologists have formed tests to assess this skill. Sometimes completed in schools, universities, or workplaces, these examinations show how advanced your spatial skills are.

Universities (chiefly manufacturing and engineering programs) frequently have their own unique spatial visualization examinations. These examinations are designed to observe students' preparedness to enter their specific program. Typically, the university suggests that students with lower scores should enroll in spatial visualization progress.

AUDITORY PROCESSING

Auditory processing has to do with the way students - in this context, teenage students, comprehend the information they hear. It is the amount and quality of understanding the students derive from a speech or any verbal expression aimed at educating them. Usually, Auditory Processing is associated with its disorder. Individuals with hearing processing disorder have a tough time hearing small sound changes in words. Someone says, "Please rise, everyone." and what a person with such disorder hear is "Please cries, hasty one" In the case of children, "Stop littering the entire place," and he might pick, "Stop flicking the necktie and plate."

Auditory Processing is anyone's ability to comprehend what they hear coherently. Still, in the case of the disorder APD, it is also known as central auditory processing disorder, is not hearing loss or a learning disorder. It means your intelligence does not 'hear' sounds in the usual way. It is not a problem with understanding meaning.

People of all ages can have APD. It usually begins at a very young age, but some people grow theirs later. Between 2% and 7% of kids have it, and boys are more likely to have it than girls. The disorder can lead to knowledge delays, so teenagers who have it may need a little extra help in the department. The condition may be linked to other things that cause similar symptoms. It is usually part of the reason some people have dyslexia. Some experts even think children are sometimes diagnosed with ADHD when they have APD. They consistently mix both concepts.

This topic is relevant to our learning strategies for teenagers because of the quality of understanding when a speech is delivered matters extensively. The causes of the disorder can affect the way your child speaks as well as his ability to read, write, and spell. He may even drop the ends of verses or mix up comparable sounds.

It can also be tough for him to dialogue with other individuals. A victim may not be able to process what others are saying and come up with a response quickly or as expected.

One, who does not have the disorder, should find themselves aiming to improve.

Reminisce on vocalized commands, chiefly if there are several steps

1. Their ability to follow conversations

2. Identify where the distant sound came from

3. Understand what people say, especially in a loud place or if more than one person is talking

4. Listen to melodious tunes and transcribe the lines.

Although no right or specific cause has been found, the common reason why some may have the disorder includes the following: Head Wound, Disease. Premature birth or low weight; sometimes, it is genetic.

If you find out that you have had a similar challenge, it is best to check yourself. You can check yourself by visiting your doctor. A doctor who is an expert in this field will examine your child critically to verify how intense if there is an issue with your child. When people take shortcuts medically, they often must pay for it dearly.

Many legends in the academic fields could hardly comprehend when they were younger. Dr. Benjamin Carson was a prominent example. Young Carson could barely understand a quarter of what was being taught in the class.

In summary, auditory processing is a student's level of comprehension of an audio delivered message. It is essential that every teenager perfectly understands the topic being taught.

LEVEL OF AROUSAL

Every teenager is a lifelong learner. Humans generally are built to learn. That is the significant difference between us, humans, and other primates and animals: we have a natural intuition to be educated, and we are committed to it.

Maybe you are the kind of person who once loved learning but became disillusioned or discouraged with the times-table-chanting and poem-memorizing that you did at school. For some of you, you probably never liked learning because you think about it with the boredom that comes with official learning. Learning is not about making excellent results. It goes beyond rote memorization and useless regurgitation of facts.

If you ever want to be the best version you can be, then it is through learning that that can be achieved. Learning has a lot of potentials, aside from the fact that those who alienate themselves from the process regret it, those who engage themselves in it reap a lot of advantages. This is so because learning translates into a better output on every other level.

Gather Information to pick the best from different online platforms. These days. There are more ways to learn than ever before. If you like to gain any language knowledge, various apps like LinguaFranca and *Duolingo* would be useful to you. Future make-up artist, Do It Yourself pro, or guitar hero? YouTube is for you. If you need a qualification, you do not need to quit your job and go to university.

You have an endless array of options on subjects to learn afresh and innumerable ways to go about achieving that. Adopt the strategies recommended in this book, find events or activities that rekindle the flame of knowledge within you, ignite the fire through any means. Keep the lights shining; you stand to benefit greatly from doing this. Remember that the activities are not coincidental; they are for your benefits both now and in the nearest future.

It is never too late to learn how differently your life could be.

Engage in Positive activities: Forget the 'what.' Why do you want to learn?

Are you motivated by career advancement, finding a new job, or earning more money?

Or do you want to show yourself and your children the benefits of getting a quality education? Maybe you have always wanted to play the guitar, harp, regular trumpet, or saxophone, or take up painting, or learn French. What you do is up to you. The most important part of the process is getting a clear picture to you.

Write the reasons for sticky notes and pinch them to your fridge, your books, and your gadgets. Save a message with your 'why' on the home screen of your handset and PC. Write it anywhere that it might motivate you or drive you away from the postponement.

If you have the reasons why you are going ahead with your plans, everything else will fall into place.

Try cleaning your head of vague thoughts about you: You're not the same person who fidgeted through school for assignments, and lateness to or coordinating assemblies, and fell asleep while tending to equations in your mathematics textbook. I am not saying that you would react any differently now under similarly constrained conditions.

What is different is that you are an adult now, however, is that you can turn your attention to the things you want to learn, the authority to ask questions, and the liberty to discover a subject and panache of learning that works for you. By accepting that the limitations of childhood are what made you turn away from your integrally human love of knowledge, you are taking the first step towards rekindling that first passion.

Be specific about your choices: Some motivations will lead themselves naturally to actions: for instance, if you are planning on moving to Portugal, then it is time to start learning how to speak Portuguese. Others can be fiddlier to work out. For instance, if you want to earn more money than you are doing currently – gaining a new criterion in your academic field is a no brainer. However, if you are going to start your profession, then qualifying is less useful than having a comprehensive knowledge of your preferred trade. Enrolling to acquire knowledge for qualification is undoubtedly a commendable exercise but what is better in this activity is the understanding you gain, not the official paper qualifications after studying.

If you want to learn for learning sake, but you are not sure what to know, then take some time to explore your choices. It is an open check for you. Check within you. You can even take a yoga class or learn any new dance, try improving your stand-up comedy skill or learn to code. Go to an analyst session at your local college or community centre or examine a few of the thousands of online courses there are out there. The success time may not be predictable, but when the results appear, you stand to reap the benefits. As mentioned earlier, there are no hard and fast rules about it; you can only take the right route.

This phase summarizes that you must create the right atmosphere for your positive learning. A healthy learning environment will enable you to analyze your study topic thoroughly.

ORIENTATION

All we do during our academic years is aimed only to get ourselves orientated about the subjects we are offered. It is all about the orientation! Few educators would refute that inspired students are more comfortable to impart or that scholars who are interested in education do learn more. So how do teachers encourage their pupils? Here are some practiced, tried-and-true strategies to get your students interested in learning.

- Memorize your schoolchildren's names and use their names as often as possible.

- Plan well in advance for every class you teach; never try to wing it. If you do, the students might discover, and there your respect goes, into the dustpan.
- Pay attention to the most significant strengths and slight limitations of each of your students. Reward their strengths and strengthen their weaknesses.
- If possible, set your room in an O-shape to encourage interaction among students. It makes it easier for them to communicate with you and vice versa.
- Try different teaching methods; try combining teaching with practical, real samples in collective or joint works, etc.
- You will never know what students do not understand unless you ask them and review the learning objectives with your students. Make sure your students get themselves acquainted with what they expected to know.

- Move around the room and look into the students' eyes as you teach. They are more connected to you that way.
- Make your classes are relevant. Ensure that the pupils understand how the content of the topics relates to them and how it relates to the world about them.
- Be communicative. Express yourself and smile.
- Engage some enthusiasm into your dialogue; change your pitch, tune, capacity, and rate.
- Ensure that the tests or examinations you give to your students are contemporary. Make sure it is relevant to the lecture topic.
- Let your pupils freely discuss the ideas surrounding the issue and correct them in any case where they do not have an accurate understanding.
- At all times, make sure the students have optimum assignments to work on the topic.
- Keep eye interaction and move near your students as you relate with them.

- Provide occasions for scholars to express themselves to the class.
- Connecting to the students should be a constant habit.
- Provide constructive feedback to students while returning projects and examinations.
- Be consistent in your treatment of students.
- Make sure to involve your students in your teaching by consistently throwing questions at them. Then ask for feedback.

Reserve about 10 minutes' sequence because students sometimes have difficulty maintaining responsiveness after a lengthier period.

ATTENTION SPAN

A teenager's attention span is a crucial factor in the learning process. The quantity of time a child spends attending and accepting the teacher's effort affects how much he or she learns from the lesson.

Hyperactivity is one of the major enemies of proper attentiveness; the other is the situation. If a child is not in the mood for studying, he or she will sit idly and fantasize or talk and interrupt the rest of the class. A short devotion span has little to do with your child and more to do with their environment. A teen's attention in the classroom will affect his or her grades

A good learning atmosphere is vital; it generates an atmosphere that places children in the right mindset to study and improves attention levels. If a few kids in the class pay devotion and respond confidently, its fasteners reflect on the rest of the course.

The average attention span of a seven-year-old is from ten to twenty-six minutes, and this grows by three to six minutes every year. Teachers must identify this, so they can plan each class consequently and impart the essential part of the lesson first.

How to Develop Your Attention Span

The development of your child is the most significant thing. If you are concerned about your child's concentration in the classroom, here are a few things you can try at home.

- Set goals for practice. E.g., Read for 50 minutes without a break.

- Play games and activities that require concentration: E.g., Crosswords, word searches.
- Practice deep breathing to improve focus.

Students often scuffle to pay devotion, but when they are given a duty they view as stimulating or challenging, they are even more likely to give up before genuinely trying. For students, whose attention consistently drifts from the classroom, you may adopt the following techniques to make them remain attentive in class.

1. Take Away Graphical Distractions

When a child is belligerent with a challenging task, litter in the classroom or on the desk can make it challenging to keep his/her brain where it essentially should be. Remove unnecessary clutter and visual involvements from the terminal.

2. Handle the Time to Work in Your Favor

In many cases, this is very necessary, but if you realize that, irrespective of what you do, the kids just can't seem to stay on task, it may be time to break content into smaller time intervals. Remember, children can concentrate on one task for two to five minutes every year as they grow. For example, if you have a classroom of majorly seven-year old's, expect 13 to 33 minutes of attention for your students.

If you realize the need to fine-tune time frames for all or some of your students, then you should do so. From time to time, ask students to show what they have done so far and ask questions about what they have gained from the class. Those who have not learned anything would quickly flip through their notes to be able to provide answers. Subsequently, in anticipation of such a session, they would follow whatever is being taught.

It breaks up the task and allows children to keep working without feeling entirely stunned. Consider calling the child to your writing table for these observations. This provides the physical movement that the child needs to stay involved in and gives you the chance to observe his or her progress.

Also, be cautious about lengthy orations with kids with short devotion lengths. These children need to be kept busy with the material, so ask for answers repeatedly on the subject matter you are discussing. Even a simple question, asking for a raise of hands, can be what is required to keep schoolchildren on duty.

3. Active involvement

Teenagers who struggle with attention often do better if they are given brief breaks for lively play. Taking a break to spring an exercise ball, breaking up learning into chunks, and open-air playtimes, or providing a quick extending or jumping jacks break in the schoolroom, can all help the attention-challenged student stay focused. Opening with twenty-five minutes of active play before a challenging task can also help a child stay more involved.

4. Ensure that You Act Deliberately

Teach the students or teenagers what it means to pay attention and how it looks. Practice attentive conduct in non-threatening, non-crucial periods during the school day. Then, at intermittent intervals, practice attention breaks. Using a timer or an application on the telephone, have a signal go off during the work period, and have the child mark whether he or she was paying attention. The activity will help the student stay focused on class lessons. It will also elongate the amount of time a student spends listening or paying attention.

5. Use Division of Labor

Many people struggle to complete every task, and they end up finishing none. Can you break it into smaller portions? When the quality time has been spent on a particular work, let the student take a break, and then revisit the topic.

Teenagers with attention struggles may perform the requested task faster with this strategy than if they simply tried to finish it all in one sitting.

Some teens are going to struggle with attention more than others. As a tutor, you can take procedures to help improve meditation for your students.

6. Building IQ

Somebody can significantly build IQ by exercising it daily. It can help improve focus. Intelligence Quotient games create the avenue for a child to horn their learning abilities; it makes the child or teenager able to focus on challenges.

In summary, teenagers should pay rapt attention to their academic studies. Distractions occur in various forms; sometimes, it happens very subtly. As a tutor, you can significantly reward a teenager that overlooks distraction to focus on his or her education.

CONCEPT FORMATION

Concept formation has to do with the creation or development of an idea. A concept is a broader view that supports the unification of data into categories. For example, the notion "square" is used to describe those things that have four equivalent sides and four right angles. Thus, the idea classifies items whose properties meet the set necessities. The way teenagers learn concepts has been planned in investigational conditions using some artificial ideas such as the one mentioned earlier - "square."

Indifference, real-life, or routine perceptions have representative rather than defining features. For example, a woodpecker would be classically considered an excellent example of the concept of birds. A seagull, however, lacks an essential defining part of this category, namely the ability to fly, and thus will not be considered a strong example of a bird's type. In the same vein, many teenagers are under the impression that the house represents a squares structure with walls, windows, and a chimney that provides shelter. As they grow, the teenager's idea of the house begins to develop to include non-typical examples.

Concepts can be learned using models, highly characteristic specimens of a category— like a woodpecker earlier talked about. The other way of concept learning is through the trial-and-error technique of testing theories. People hold the presumption, or they assume that a specific item is an occurrence of a particular concept; they then learn more about the notion when they see whether their premise is accurate or otherwise.

Individuals learn artless concepts more willingly than difficult ones. For example, the most straightforward concept to grasp is one with only a single crucial feature. The next therefore is one with multiple components, all of which must be current in every case, known as the conjunctive idea. In this idea, there are links in all the required attributes. It is more challenging to master a so-called disjunctive theory when either one feature or another must be present. Teenagers also learn concepts, in general, more quickly when provided with both options but with a positive rather than a negative image of a picture in mind.

Summarily, teenage students aspiring to learn better should adopt the style of forming concepts. Every topic is based on the expansion of an idea; those who detect ways to develop concepts get more familiar with the subject.

SOCIAL CONDUCT

Our social conduct goes a long way in determining how much we know. Even children from a very early age are taught to be fair and kind to others regardless of their age and their relationship with them. These are not on the platter of coincidental goodwill. When in school, teenagers often reflect their acts of sharing or kindness in their natural behavior, like when they are having lunch or helping someone in doing their homework. When good behavior is prized, it has a ripple effect on the child's character and his or her positive social conduct. Appreciation, authentic praise, and compliments boost the self-assurance and lift a general sense of pleasure in them. Happy students are more likely to perform satisfactorily in their institute.

Some of the good conducts are:

Appreciation

Think about it. There are several things in the world today, some of which are very beautiful, and they still affect our lives positively. Young children indeed place high regard for their teachers, and it is this very sensation that makes the teachers accountable for acknowledging their student's efforts and making them comprehend the prominence of expressing gratitude. Teachers should express appreciation in public because it lifts happy thoughts in the school children. You can either ask the students to maintain a journal or place a notice board where the students and the teachers can openly stick notes of gratitude, which are on exhibition for all and sundry, sending a positive vibe across the hall for the achiever and the receiver.

Empathy by Reflection

Teenagers need to feel cherished, protected and safeguarded to partake in pro-social conduct inside or outside school. As a teacher or a parent or a guardian, you should attempt to make one on one expressive relationship with kids.

Science has proven that teenagers with a good moral compass are academically brighter.

INTERPERSONAL SKILLS

Interpersonal skills include many things. They are those which help a person communicate well. Interpersonal skills imply that communication takes place between two persons. Unlike monologues, more than one person is required to establish interpersonal communication. When you have two or more people communicating, then the communication is said to be interpersonal. The communication can be expressed non-verbally or through gestures, verbally (i.e., speaking through the mouth), through eye moments, nuances, signals, or different postures. Of course, communication has to do with understanding the common subject which themes the speakers' conversation.

Without the same field of experience, the interpersonal communiqué would not happen. While the possession of this skill does come with ease, following a pattern can make it easy for just about anyone who tries it.

Learning involves trying to understand the interest and fields of individuals. It is essential because it takes knowing people to understand them better. From a distance, a lot of wrong assumptions could be made, with other indicators to back them up, but when we speak with people, we get to know them for who they are. The more you try and understand the background of the people, their interest, and the foundation, the easier it will be for you to communicate, as well. Always try to strike up conversations with as many people as you get the chance. The importance of this action is getting to know people better and not judging them based on unfounded assumptions.

SELF EXPRESSION

The expression is a powerful character. It may seem like an attribute of teaching rather than learning, but one needs it just as much. Asking a simple question after a long tutorial requires the ability to be self-expressive. Cirss Jami once said that "Everyone has their ways of expression. I trust we all have a lot to say but discovering means to say it is extra than half the urge."

Imagine if you could liberally and unabashedly express who you are and what you want?

Self-expression is an integral part of sharing our assistance and talents with the world. It is how we share what is important to us, what we believe in, and what we desire.

Self-expression is how we link with each other more intensely. It allows us to know-how empathy and understanding so we can help and serve others.

It is vital to have an avenue to express ourselves and let our character shine freely. If we do not feel comfortable expressing ourselves, it will be hard to show up fully, be bold, and make a difference in the world. If we do not believe we have a voice worth heeding, we would not speak up or prompt our needs, hopes, and thoughts.

Ways to Express Yourself Better

1. **Speak Up!** Some people have a hard time speaking up. They feel nervous and shy and lack self-assurance in what they want to say. They have remained shut down and misjudged, and because of this, have ceased from speaking up. It takes practice and courage, but you can grow your sureness around speaking your mind. You can join a book or reading group where everyone shares their thoughts and opinion about a book collectively read. You can join or attend

speaking programs, such as Mashturancou Intercontinental and Mega WWRI; these will teach you to speak more decently, directly, and assuredly. Consider the advantages embedded in it when you can create opportunities to speak publicly and open your vocal cords.

Self-expression is how much we are understood and share who we are with the world. There are many ways to express ourselves. Choose one of the ideas above and practice sharing your thoughts, feelings, and dreams through these means. Do not judge or critique your capability. Try to be open and at liberty. Trust the route and allow your self-expression to bud. Keep in mind that it was through learning that you acquired knowledge in the first instance.

2. Be Trendy: Dance and Enjoy the Happening Fun

Dancing and body movement is a very complicated form of self-expression. The act of twirling and physique movement is inborn and occurs worldwide. Even a toddler can sense tempo and express this feeling through effort. Our conduct and body language are an addition to speaking and self-expression.

In dancing and drive is the capability to feel extensive and let go of the narrowing feelings that keep us inflexible and unresponsive. Our actions are also organized with our reactions and can be used to swing our mindset and approach. That is why social psychologist Professor Mendel Ashton encourages people to use power posing to feel more confident and reduce stress. Whether you power stance or rave, play about with expressing your feelings through movement. Chant and play a good melody. One of the most common ways to describe how we feel and who we are is through listening and or singing songs. Even if you are feeling pleased on a deep summer day or depressed and unhappy on a cold winter day, the mood can request the kind of song it wants to hear. Your body can tell you if you listen to it. You can even compose one if the desired tone is not immediately available.

3. Penning down Your Thoughts: Many people discover it convenient to express themselves through some form of inscription. Whether you write prose, poetry, novels, novellas, songs, or simply journal about yourself or others, articulating yourself through writing can help you share your opinions, feelings, and viewpoint. Just make sure you allot time to writing every blessed day. You can get more precise and start inscription about your life experiences. It could be your earliest memory from a nursery or an experience you had in the very recent past.

4. Build a Clothing Pattern that Suits Your Style: There are a lot of people who do not care about sticking to a style. However, it is always respectable to wear outfits that showcase your inner beauty. The best thing is to adopt a pattern that will speak for you before you are addressed.

SELF CONTROL

Discipline is the most crucial guide for anyone who truly wants to succeed at anything. Having self-control is not as simple as it sounds. A lot goes into it. Here are three areas of self-control and how we all might struggle with them. To have self-control is to be in absolute control of the things that happen around you and to be in control of your reactions to those things. Rather than taking actions that would embarrass you, such steps as speaking out of turn, interrupting others, missing out on points that other people are making in a conversation, talking too much and being consistently called to caution, or giving false accounts while speaking. Others are not get started on homework until close to bedtime, Rush through assignments, follow the rules one day but not the next, and lack emotional control. Self-Control is the ability of an individual to manage feelings. You have more control of raw emotions such as hunger, drive, and urges, etc.

Displays of lack of self-control are:

1. Have a hard time calming down to get things done, such as chores, and not handle disagreements well.

2. Get easily frustrated and give up

3. Disrupt games and conversations with their movements

4. Have trouble keeping their cool when someone upsets or annoys them

5. Lack of restrictions on people.

6. Handling fragile items carelessly.

7. Unnecessarily embarrassing yourself and others.

8. Have trouble sitting still

9. Inability to maintain being cool.

10. Damaging things before you realize.

To develop your self-control ability, you may need to get an honest assessment from the people around you. You should ask them to make recommendations in their review too so that you will learn how to improve your lifestyle better.

In conclusion, this chapter explains the importance of having self-control on a teenager's academic performance. Self-control drives the student to deny himself of several pleasures from his or her comfort zone to put in more effort on what will yield positive results academically.

SHARING/TURN TAKING

Sharing and Turn-taking is substantially affected by the nature of exchange. As we have seen so far in this activity of learning how to learn, purely transactional interactions (such as many service encounters) do not require high-level turn-taking skills. However, informal conversations are another matter altogether.

The nature of casual conversation has been quite methodically investigated, and various authors have suggested what the defining characteristics are of such encounters; casual conversation does not follow a set task. Neither side of such exchanges has a particular end in sight; no agenda is set. Compare this, for example, to a workplace meeting which may, indeed, be informal and entail good turn-taking skills but which will also have some schedule to follow and duty to accomplish, however imprecisely that is restricted. This is a catalog rather than a style issue, but they are linked types.

Authority relationships tend to be appropriately alike. If they are not, chance-taking continues rather inversely with one person suggesting not only whose turn is next but also what the topic of the arch will involve. Unfairness in participation is often a feature of some registers – learning, decision-making, administrational, roles, etc. There are usually a small number of contributors. Even in school settings, during extra curriculum activities or informal conversations, tend to be in small groups of merely three to five people. Whatever larger and we are in the territories of dialogues or entire speeches which, asides from interrupting from the floor, do not usually necessitate any turn-taking strategies.

Therefore, based on the kind of turn-taking skills you want to impart, grow and exercise, you need to make sure that the situation in which performance and rehearsal take place is harmonized with the kinds of skill you want to be the emphasize.

PROCRASTINATION

How does procrastination affect the learning capability of a teenager?

Consider this: You have a massive plan for you, but you do not disturb yourself over them because you know there is always time to attend to them. Before anything else, you suddenly realize that the day is over already. All the time you thought you would follow to things just vanished before you even had time to think about them. It is also a theoretically hazardous force, causing sufferers to fail out of educational line, and it affects their general performances. It also relaxes medical treatment and delays any possible savings. A circumstance Western Reserve University study from 1997 found that college-age procrastinators ended up with higher stress, more illness, and lower results by the end of the semester. Deferment affects many people, thwarting them from completing their most vital and essential responsibilities, but the reasons people adjourn are not understood that well.

An investigation into the beginning of procrastination will expose that it is difficult to find a root. Most psychologists see procrastination as a kind of evasion behavior; It usually happens when people fear or dread, or have concerns about, the important task awaiting them. To get rid of this destructive sensation, people adjourn duties — they settle for Play Station 5 instead, and sooner than they know it, the time has elapsed. That makes them feel better temporarily, but regrettably, reality comes back to bite them in the end.

In the face of realistic deadlines, guilt, and shame accompanies procrastination. But for an extreme procrastinator, those negative feelings can be just another reason to put the task off, with the behavior turning into a malicious, self-defeating sequence.

Delivering yourself from procrastination requires a good dose of self-discipline. You must follow the five following steps:

1. Do it as soon as it comes to your mind: The moment in-between procrastination and failure does not exist. To avoid late remembrance, do the plans as soon as it comes to mind.

2. Consistently Check if there are leftovers: Before you sleep, try to reflect on all the things you planned to do if there are any you did not attend to, it is the best time to attend to them if that is possible quickly.

3. Get a Reminder/Memo/Diary: Write down all you plan and date them. If you find yourself struggling with fulfilling your plans, then you should have them on record. Records help you remember those plans and attend to them in good time.

4. Inform Others: By getting people to hold you to ransom, you find yourself fulfilling the plans quickly to be a disciplined person.

5. **Avoid Doing All:** Give yourself space. Do not subject yourself to fulfilling everything on your list. No one can do everything in the world; do not try to be the first. If you do, you will sooner than later wear yourself out. Cross out your plans before you realize that you are not able to fulfill them and inform the necessary people immediately you do so.

PLAY

Playing is not only the coolest thing we find ourselves engaging in, but it is one of the most beneficial activities that are available in the universe today. Long term learning also involves a lot of playing too. All work without play, as is popularly quoted, makes Jack a dull boy. That does not apply to Jack alone but to everyone who is denied the time to play.

Playing does not have anything to do with age. Everyone should have a chance to express themselves most energetically freely they know how to. That comes with a great sensation of happiness, freedom, and enjoyment. A child who has deliberate time to play find it easier to focus on learning than a child who has been restricted from playing. The play has no limitations and can be anything ranging from goofing off with friends, cracking jokes with fellow workers, or hurling a Frisbee at a friend on the beach, building a snowman in the yard, playing fetch with a dog, or going for a bike ride with your peers. There does not need to be any point to the activity beyond having fun and enjoying yourself.

However, too much of everything has its evil sides. Playing likewise, a child who is more engaged in playing would inevitably find it difficult to focus on actual learning—in that regard, playing needs to be curbed and curtailed by a parent or guardian.

Advantages of playing

While the play is crucial for a teenager's development and academic assimilation, it is also helpful for people of all ages. Fun can contribute joy to life, relieve stress, supercharge education, and attach you to others and the world around you. Play can also make work more creative and enjoyable. You can play either on your own or with a pet animal. Still, for the greatest benefit, you should involve at least a person and play away from the sensory burden of electronic gadgets. Playing soccer, chess, skating or completing puzzles, or pursuing other fun activities that test the brain can help avert memory difficulties and improve brain tasks. It enhances brain utility. The social collaboration of playing with family and friends can also help ward off stress and despair.

As much as playing gives a lot of fun, it can also trigger the release of endorphins, which are the body's natural feel-good chemicals. Endorphins, produced by playing, develop an individual's wellbeing state and this is mentally and medically relieving. When you play, you are rid of stress and tension. You can also improve relationships and your connection to others. Sharing laughter and fun can foster kindness, understanding, faith, and familiarity with the people around us. Play does not have to include a specific activity; it can merely also be a state of mind. Developing a playful nature can help you undo stressful or tense situations, form new business relationships, make new friends, and break the ice with strangers or engage in any other more creative thing.

Keep feeling young and energetic. Playing develops vitality and even advance your resistance to disease, helping you function at your best irrespective of your age.

Stimulate the mind and boost creativity. Teenagers often learn best when they are playing—a principle that relates to adults, as well. You will understand a new task better when it is fun, and you are in a relaxed and playful mood. Playing can also kindle your resourcefulness, helping you familiarize and resolve difficulties.

Play is one of the most operative apparatuses for keeping associations renewed and exhilarating. Playing together brings happiness, energy, and pliability to relationships. Play can also heal hatred, differences, and pains. Through consistent performance, we learn to trust one another and feel harmless. Hope allows us to work together, open ourselves to familiarity, and try new things. By building attentive resolve to include more humor and play into your everyday relations, you can advance the value of your love interactions—as well as your acquaintances with neighbours, friends, and associates.

Collaborative skills are learned as part of the give and take of play. During the teenage years of play, kids learn about verbal communication, body language, boundaries, cooperation, and cooperation. As adults, you continue to improve these abilities through play and playful interactions. Play teaches collaboration with others. Play is a powerful substance for optimistic socialization.

This chapter projects the importance of not staying docile while learning. Teenagers who spend time to have fun or play games while focusing on academic break timeframe are better at their learning performance.

POSTURE

Everyone needs to be well-positioned to live well. For teenagers aspiring to learn, the topic is just as relevant. In soccer, for instance, the goalkeeper must be well-positioned to avoid the calamitous score from a free-kick from an opponent. The same principle applies. Young children and students carry on to spending more and more time at a desk for schoolwork, especially typing.

It is vital to take regular breaks – at least every thirty minutes to stand and stretch. It is essential not only for the collar and back muscles but also to prevent eye exhaustion. Set a regulator on your handset to remind you to stretch every 30 minutes. Here are some simple tips to note.

Nudge position – Make sure your elbows are close to the body; angle is open about 85-125 degrees

Wrist position – Wrist is nonaligned and leveled with forearms

Spinal cord supported by the chair – Sitting up conventionally, with the spine supported, body in front of the keyboard, if working on the computer.

Head position – Head positioning is essential; in a neutral position (or slightly advancing), position your head to be in line with the chest.

Hip position – Hips at about 90-100 degrees

Knee position – Keep knees at about 90-100 degrees

Flat feet – Feet are to be flatly placed on the floor

Optionally, lift your workstation so you can stand and work to differ your positions without stress.

To avoid neck injuries while carrying out some functions, then it is best to exercise your neck consistently. It is a term to describe neck pain from continually leaning over your handset to type, attend to your social media handles or watch videos and skits. Everyone is guilty of it from time to time, but it is essential to develop healthy posture habits when using any kind of handset, especially a smartphone. Text collar can cause neck pain and may have potential long-term effects. Yoga springs may provide relief or lessen the discomfort and inspire good posture moving onward.

In summary, posture plays an essential role in learning. An experienced teacher can quickly figure out if you are focusing or not keen on the subject merely by looking at your posture.

REHEARSAL

Especially for young people, rehearsals are essential to learning. Some useful tips for rehearsing include the following:

1. Competence: You get to learn about each other better. If, for example, someone forgets a part and must improvise, in a choir setting, for example, by making eye contact, everyone knows what they need to do to fix the problem. It is that easy after training to become competent. As a result, the viewers would not see the fault.

2. Melody: You learn to develop a song to its fullest prospective by creating tempo, arrangements, and tone selections, which all affect the delivery of the music.

3. Believe as You Aspire: Each practice must be born out of the passion for getting better. If your mind has already defeated you, you cannot overcome your physical appearance. A little exercise of the body will give a great reflection of surrounding greatness.

4. *Continue Doing the Right Thing*: One of the most obvious reasons is that no one can improve their craft without working hard to get better. Even the world's best musicians practice every day.

5. *Group Work*: It is a popular fact that engaging in group work helps to create something with a more remarkable impression. Hearing people's opinions and trying out new things that you may not have been aware of can make a huge difference.

In summary, daily practice is a perfect strategy for learning during your teenage years. You need to be consistent to achieve whatever learning goal you have set for yourself to succeed.

ORGANIZATION SKILLS

Teenagers aspiring to employ the best strategies for learning must adopt good organizational skills. Good organization skills make the teen look responsible and attractive. To attain a high level of organization skills, you must be vast in the following:

1. Time Efficiency and Delegation: Failure in this area will lead to you being unable to stay on the task in front of you. Leaders must strictly adhere to a disciplined pattern of action. It would be hard to trust a leader or teacher who finds it challenging to keep to time. List out your daily plans and work by them. Check yourself from time to time to see how well you adhere to your plans.

2. Controlling Your Activities by Sticking to Your Defined Strategies: Remember that planning takes different forms, including dealing with time and how a project must proceed.

3. Thorough Preparation: Thorough Preparation indicates to others that you have awareness about what they are doing. Thanks to Thorough preparation, your understanding of the time taken for different aspects becomes improved.

4. Utilization of Surrounding Advantages: Utilization in this sense means being acutely aware of the resources at hand. People are always drawn toward those who have excellent organization skills. Following the methods mentioned earlier would keep you well-positioned for good learning.

LEARNING STYLES

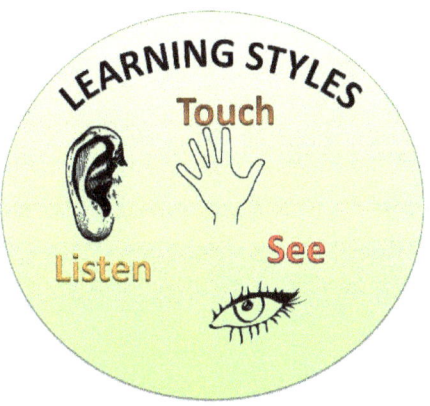

One of the essential tactics to learn better for any teenager involves adopting proper learning styles. The learning process consists of a lot of physical, mental, and emotional engagement. You can build every aspect of this by developing the following sections.

1. Pictorial: Take into perception, a pictorial learner in an inscription class, he may process the data well by seeing a flick of clips of what the entire talk is about. A picture, as they say, is a million words. In the case of such people under this category, that is just very true.

2. Aural/Auditory learners: People who fall in this category learn quickly by listening. It might take a long time for them to process information presented through verbal teachings or pictorial means.

3. Physical Learners (commonly called Kinesthetic): Have you ever met anyone who enjoys getting their hands working on whatever they come across? Then you have likely encountered a physical learner. People in this category like to learn through practice. When the teacher makes the pupils get their hands dirty through practical lectures, such students are usually ahead of the class.

When you understand the kind of learner you are, it would be easy to identify what works best for you. You are a Visual person who assimilates better through reading, or you are a listener or a practical person. You can be the best in your style.

STUDY DURATION

The amount of time you exploit studying has a lot to do with how much you achieve from the book learning process. It is using your time productively and competently—but what about when you are working as productively as possible, and you still cannot get everything done? It may be better to think about Study Duration as a mixture of working productively and prioritizing your time. Study Duration is the ability to use your time effectively and efficiently. You could also think of it as the art of needing time to do everything that you want without feeling stressed about it. It sounds simple, but it is much harder in exercise. This page explains some of the values behind good Study Duration. Study Duration skills are essential because few, if any, of us ever have enough time to do everything possible of us or that we want to do.

In other words, people who are good at their study duration are good at getting and doing things promptly. They are also, however, better at prioritizing and working out what needs to be done—and then discarding the other things that might serve as a distraction.

They can do this because they understand the difference between urgent and essential. Urgency is required to conquer critical tasks. You need to give yourself the time-space necessary to attend to duties before they become embarrassing and urgent.

When you spend so much studying, likely, you will soon perfect your understanding of the content you are reading from. Some people grab things faster than others, but any consistent person has an edge.

Remember that what you occupy your mind with goes a long way. Once you spend quality time studying, you become familiar with the topic, and you perfect your knowledge of it.

A great way to learn through utilizing time is by finding fun while you study.

If you like being with people, then you could consider study partners who would help you discuss topics that you need to know. Following this pattern, you will realize that you can spend all your time studying. All it takes is remembering the reward that comes with it.

This chapter talks about time efficiency. Utilizing time is essential for any good learner.

CONCLUSION

Nothing guarantees excellence in any learning performance, other than the strategies discussed in this book, met with a willing heart. As much as the recommendations in the books are a thousand percent reliable, it all starts with a heart that is willing to learn. Such willingness alone births the adoption of effective learning strategies, as has been judiciously treated in this book.

The greatest men in the universe today have succeeded in all fields because of their continuous dedication to whatever they found themselves doing. However, none of them bypassed the learning process.

Life itself has shown that the better learning strategies a person adopts, the more guaranteed such a person's success. Knowing this as a teenager promises a great lot of good happening in the future.

Education is a lifelong process. Our education system prepares us for skills that we need to learn, but it does not teach "How to learn." Everyone is unique, and so is their environment. "One size fits all approach does not work as everyone has different styles and methods of learning.

Our goal in this book is to empower the reader to learn about the components that affect our learning. This book will help the reader to improvise their learning skills.

Homeschooling is becoming common these days, and that puts pressure on students to learn by themselves. It is becoming essential that people identify different components of learning and use it to their benefit.

www.ingramcontent.com/pod-product-compliance
Lightning Source LLC
Chambersburg PA
CBHW041957080526
44588CB00021B/2772